A Frozen World

Adult Coloring Book Penguins Edition

Coloring Bandit

Published by Speedy Publishing Canada Limited

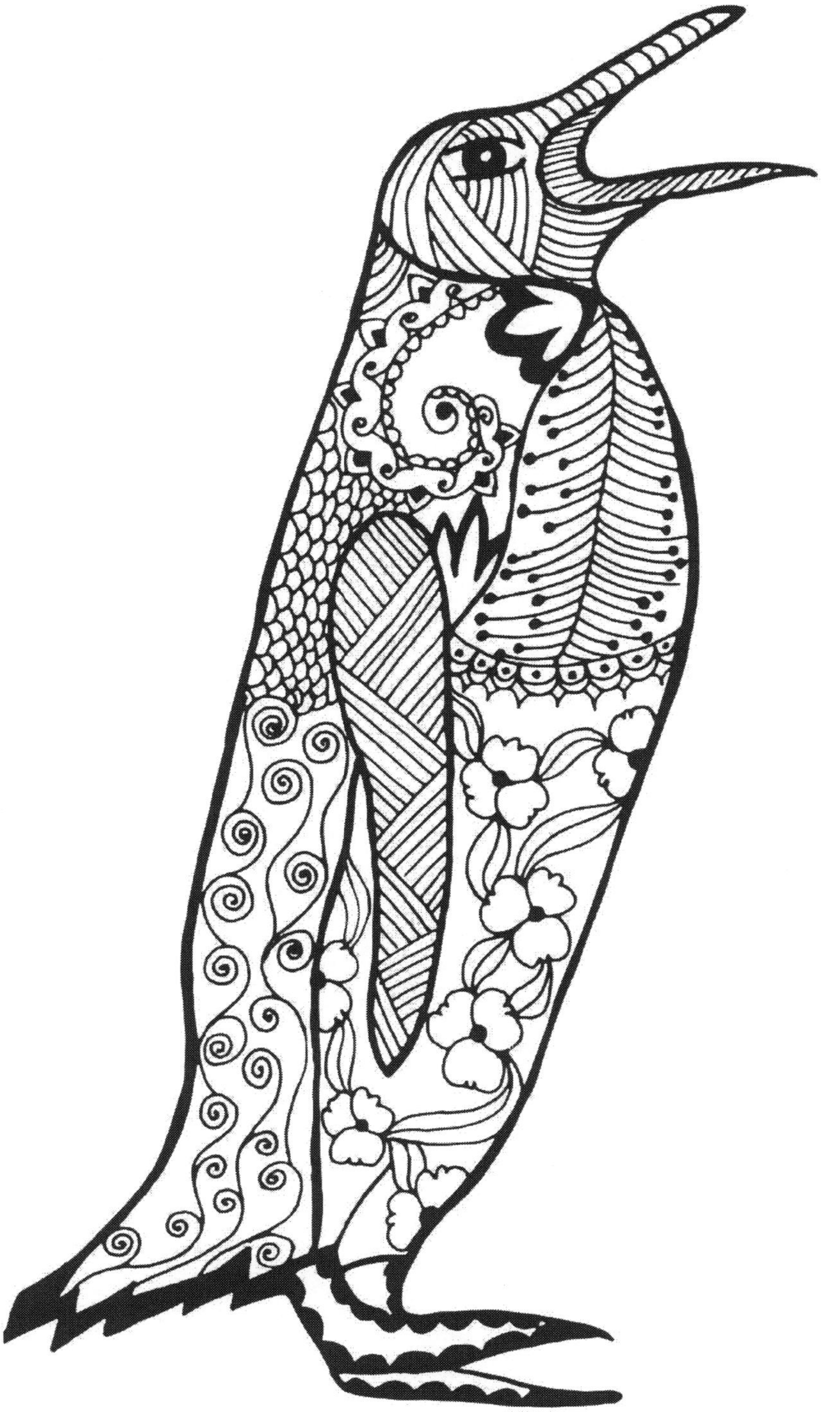

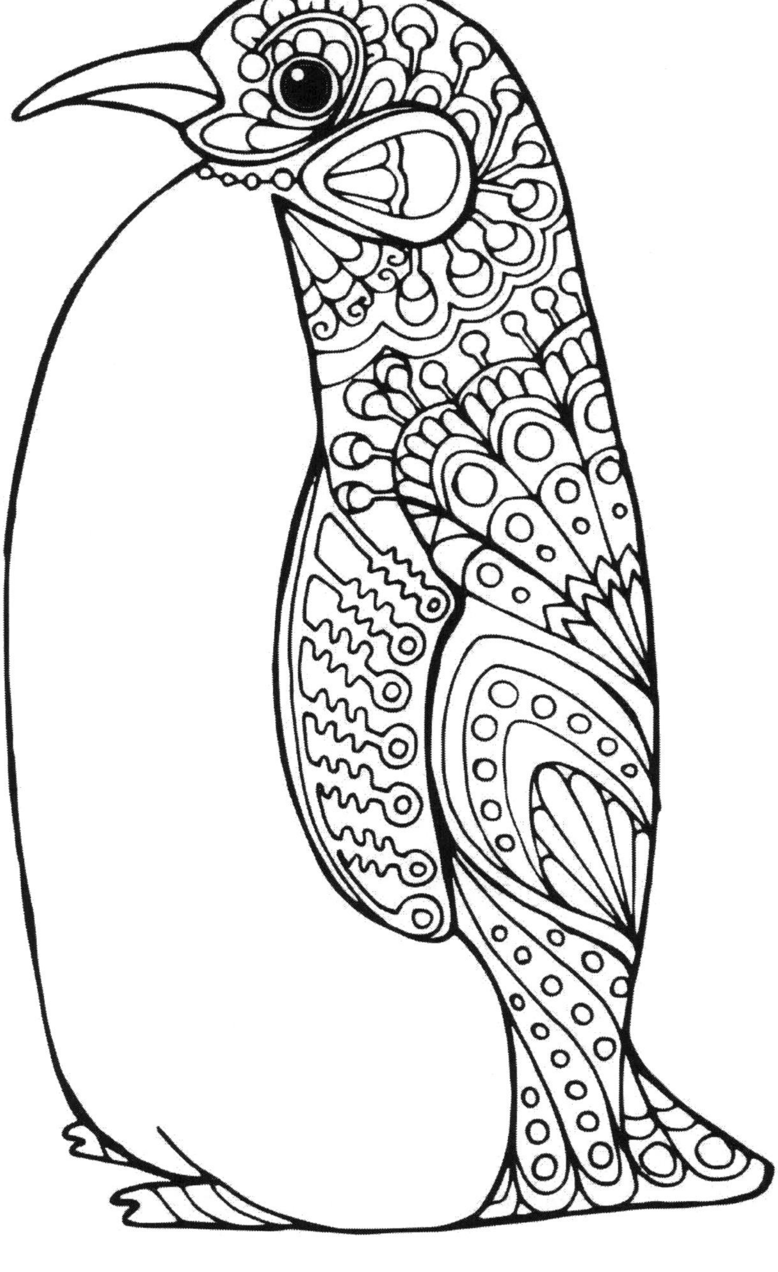

This is a Bleed Through Page If You Are Using a Colouring Marker or Pen!
Find Other Great Titles By searching for Coloring Bandit on Your Favorite Book Retailer
Amazon.Ca | Barnes & Noble (BN.Com) | Books A Million (BAM.Com)

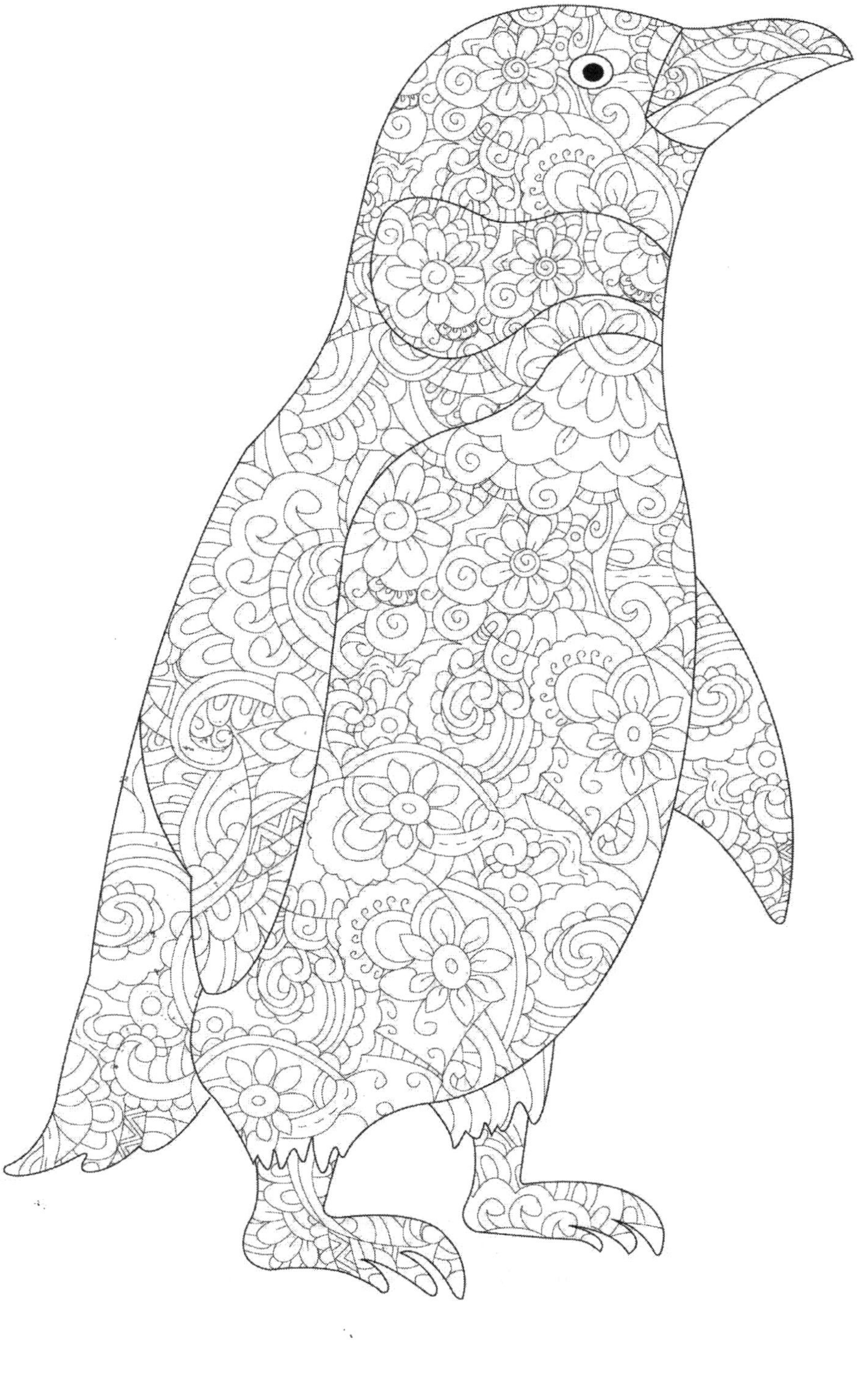

This is a Bleed Through Page If You Are Using a Colouring Marker or Pen!

This is a Bleed Through Page If You Are Using a Colouring Marker or Pen!

Find Other Great Titles By searching for Coloring Bandit on Your Favorite Book Retailer

Amazon.Ca | Barnes & Noble (BN.Com) | Books A Million (BAM.Com)

COLORING BANDIT

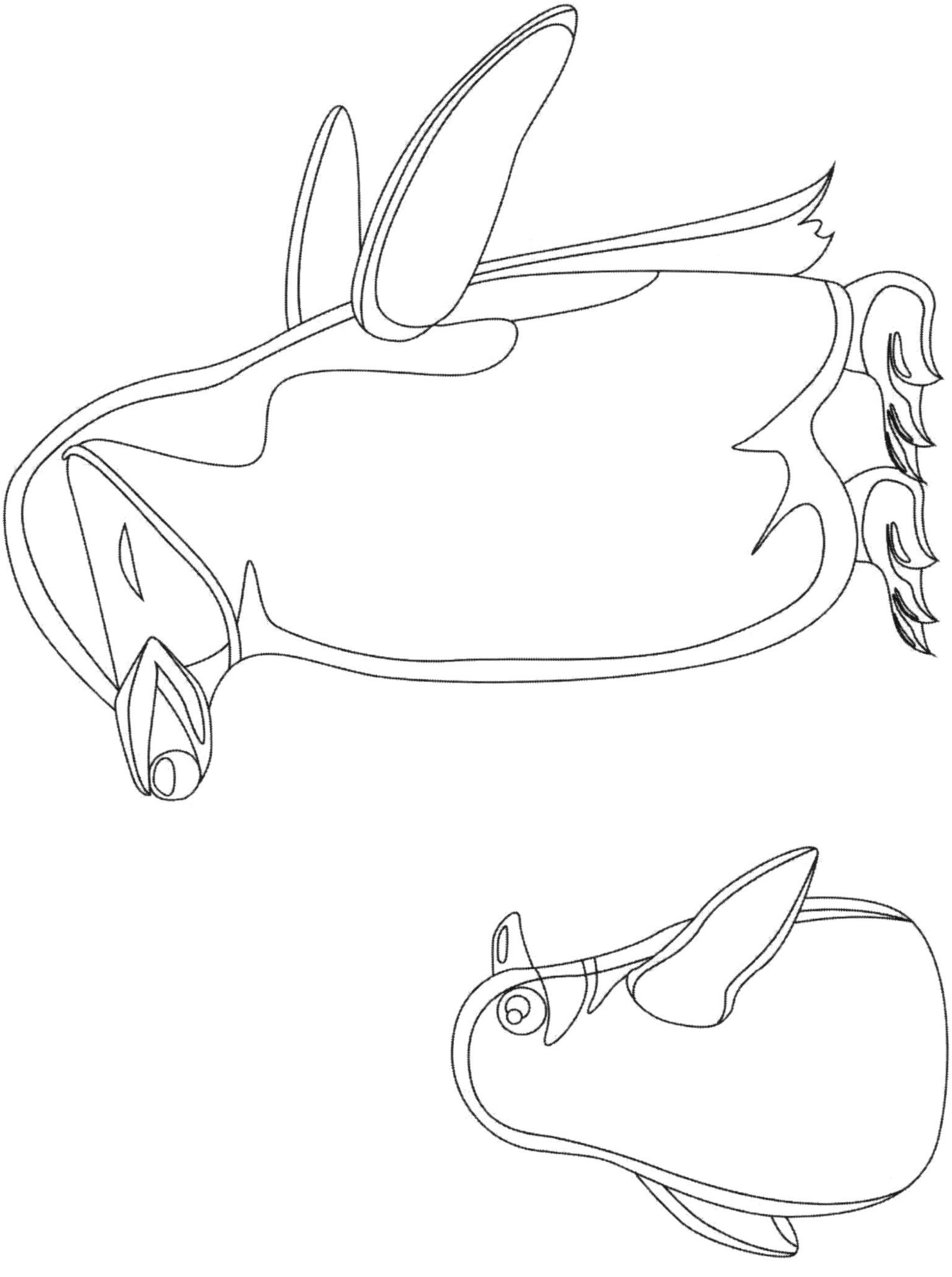

13682795R00035

Made in the USA
Middletown, DE
18 November 2018